Jeopardy

Gregory Warren Wilson

Jeopardy

ENITHARMON PRESS

First published in 2003
by the Enitharmon Press
26B Caversham Road
London NW5 2DU

www.enitharmon.co.uk

Distributed in the UK by
Central Books
99 Wallis Road
London E9 5LN

Distributed in the USA and Canada
by Dufour Editions Inc.
PO Box 7, Chester Springs
PA 19425, USA

ISBN 1 900564 63 7

Enitharmon Press gratefully acknowledges the
financial support of Arts Council England

British Library Cataloguing-in-Publication Data.
A catalogue record for this book is available
from the British Library

Typeset in Bembo by Servis Filmsetting Ltd
and printed in England by
Antony Rowe Ltd

for Peter Davie

ACKNOWLEDGEMENTS

I would like to thank the editors of the following publications in which some of these poems, or earlier versions of them, first appeared: *Coast to Coast Competition Anthology 1997*; *Frogmore Papers*; *The Interpreter's House; Orbis*; *PHRAS 97 Anthology; Poetry, the 21st Century* (Japan, translated Mikiko Iida); *Smiths Knoll; Soundings; Staple; Tears in the Fence; Thumbscrew; Vision On; Departures* (ed. Kate Shaw, The Housman Society); *Eating Your Cake . . . and Having It* (ed. Ann Gray, Fatchance Press).

'The Invisible Colourist' won the Coast to Coast National Writing Competition.

'Foreign Tongue' was a prize winner in the PHRAS 97 Open Poetry Competition.

I am grateful to Joyce Coleman for the quotation on page 99, and for her steadfast encouragement.

I would like to thank Carole Satyamurti for her insight and critical generosity over the years. I would also like to thank Mark Kilfoyle for his way of opening my eyes to books, and books to my eyes.

CONTENTS

JEOPARDY

STAGED WHISPERS

Because I cannot sleep
I make music at night.

Rumi

JEOPARDY

Space enclosed between these leaves
has changed, has been defined
by sculptures that are no longer here.

Trees that seemed to have little to do
with the lost-wax process, now stand
in relation to more than one another.

Something still remains, as if visible
to the ear, audible to the skin. Here
not only vacancy has been disclosed;

a tangible mirage of air has replaced
bronze and lichen coloured patinas,
making apprehensible the specific

gravity of silence, and the fluent
volume of space I occupied, but now
have left forever closing behind me.

My wife, of course, was none too keen.
Mattar panir she said, *with Emmenthal?*
And nowhere to buy fresh coriander I bet.
Particle physicists don't have much choice
where to work. So we went.

The apartments all seemed much the same;
we took one on the fourth floor, for the view
into leaves. 'Cream rugs . . . from India,'
the agent smiled. Quite by chance.

The first evening, melting ghee
in an unaccustomed pan,
even the snowflakes surrendered
to my wife's aromatic touch;
dal tarka, aloo bhaji, paratha
rustled up out of thin air.
We were relieved, and lit incense.
Later she said *That bathroom*
has all the charm of a kidney dish
and unbraided her hair.

Two children, Aadam and Jamila,
both quick with languages.
We'd call to them in Hindi,
they'd answer in English, or Punjabi.
Swiss–German didn't seem a barrier.

Then the tapping began.
Tap tap tap on the radiator pipes.
Tap tap tap tap *tap.*

My wife looked at me, shushed the children.
Their giggles, suppressed, turned hysterical,
erupted into squeals. Tap tap tap.
Aadam started to dance –
more Shiva than Fred Astaire.

I put on my jacket and went down.
He answered the door like a holy man
aflame. I said, *I understand Morse code*
kept prisoners sane in the camps, but we . . .

From the doorway I could see
a Chardin still life of partridges
and a spiky little Klee.
It was not, as the English say, the moment.

'Isn't this block unsuitable for you
to bring up your children? Don't
they need a garden for their trampoline?'
All his windows were closed.

When I returned, my wife was pale
with chickpea flour.

to keep by you. To remember me by.
Provisions for a journey. Take them

simply as I take pleasure in giving
these speckled beauties from the hens

you came to know by name: *Sappho, the Cropper,
Eyebright, Dido, the Lame Comedienne.*

There's nothing, almost nothing, like
a bloodwarm egg at rest in your palm.

My love, wherever you're going, remember
the Gods are charmed by humble offerings –

a crocus on a makeshift altar,
a saucer of milk, the goatherd's song –

and remember waking beside me here
with the hens, the early sun all yolk

and a trace of white still on our skins . . .

British Museum; Greek, 5th century BC

FIELD OF VISION

What happens to shadows when the light
absents itself? Is there a gathering up
of the indistinct, like pastry scraps
to make one sharp-edged leaf or lattice?

And the volume in this enamel bowl:
was it always present, if only now
made visible, defined by the meniscus
of emptiness brimming lip to lip?

Why ask . . . once having seen
a patch of yellow – yellow grass
stencilled where a tent was staked
and then the whole field entirely

free from contingency: no haze
of unsown flax, no subtle after-
image contradicting the retina;
nothing less than this sufficiency

– dazzling plain, green, utterly.

Would he have left by now, my perfect
lover – considerate, laboriously discreet,
careful not to ruck the skin of sleep
in case I, in the half-light, detect
how susceptible affinity can be? If woken
inadvertently, might I locate some defect,
being the less ardent? If there's a fault,
isn't it the dullness love assumes, once spoken?

How quickly we become strange
to one another; how quickly we intimate
the phases of this impulse to consummate
desire. If I could, would I rearrange
the numbers on the clock, reset the alarm
to suit myself, and in so doing estrange
each of us from the other, and the dawn? Let
time save us from doing more – more harm.

Better to catch myself in the act
of conjuring shadow into form – a glimpse
of his flesh sheathed again, one wrist
tightening the other's strap – than react
to his departure. Could I have slept
if he'd so much as moved? The fact
that a dream is so easily feigned meant
I could watch him as he dressed and left

– nothing: no phone number, not a word,
no stolen first edition or opened page,
not even a cup in the kitchen rearranged.
Listening through half-closed eyes I heard
the emptiness begin to fill, like a courtyard
with sleepy birds, my inner ear turned inward
on itself as if to overhear the counterpoint
to a part I hadn't learned; a lament, an aubade.

Night, like a handful of ink in the sea,
dissipates; will some salty essence endure
a little longer on air and skin before
withdrawing with the tide? Is constancy
sustained by flux, as flight is by wings
being flexed? What would he forego, or foresee?
Would he leave me the moon? Having no light
of its own, it silently reflects on things.

When people ask me what I *do* I say
   Imagine a glasshouse where orchids and cacti
   bloom in black and white:
   I colour them in, just as I please,
but it is not quite like that.

I'm working on a ballet score.
Big commission. Manila packages arrive
for me to orchestrate – minute by minute.
Composers know just how long it takes;
times like this I'm indispensable,
fleshing out their wire-frame staves.
A piano score's a meagre thing
but I have learnt how not to overstep
the mark.

Sometimes I blend a clarinet duet
low in the *chalumeau* (molten white chocolate)
with *divisi* violas; sometimes I hazard
a harp *glissando* (a salon touch)
and risk a frisson of *tremolo*,
but my range is always defined
by somebody else's double bar. I
remain veiled – a ghost, a *doppelgänger*.

Yes I used to compose, but now my skill
is more exact, more exacting. It's a rare gift,
this feel for anonymity while taking pride
in expertise; *that* you can quantify –
crafting a phrase around the bassoon's
break, laying out page turns,
giving the oboist a split
second to moisten the cor anglais reed.

What they want of me goes unspoken —
to merge like mercury, skin into skin,
till I disappear, acoustically.

I live on my own in a quiet bit of Hove;
most afternoons I collect cork floats,
flints that fit in the palm, cuttlebone.
No one comes anywhere near
Debussy's scoring of *La Mer* —
not Britten, or Vaughan Williams; he
keeps the tam-tam in reserve . . . Like the tide

I've learnt to withdraw — to leave
my work to be appraised,
and if a passage has to be re-thought
the acetates can be wiped clean
with alcohol — just as waves will rinse away
gull-prints and the sand's graffiti.
Selfless as that. Nearly.

I am sick sick sick sick sick of being fobbed off
with snuffboxes, enamel trinkets and watches
one after another instead of my proper fee.

What need have I for a clock in every pocket
repeating on me, *me* – the finest timekeeper of all –
all Mannheim at least? Punctuality. It does nothing

but demean. Oh there are nights when the whole sky
revolves like a timepiece in my hand, when constellations
suspend themselves in a matrix of silence,

patient as icicles waiting to melt into sound.
You know how sometimes a fugue presents itself
and all its possibilities in an instant . . . ?

I wear myself out, working out the workings of each
inevitability: the balance wheel, the hairspring coiled
like a butterfly's tongue, the jewelled intricacies.

Tonight it's freezing – all glockenspiel and glass
harmonica, inaudible to everyone but me,
and I must single-handedly transcribe the stars,

must find each one its place in these ruled staves,
must bring down the chiming of the spheres
and shackle the celestial in inky rings –

minim and semibreve. Must put heaven behind bars.
Being human – utterly, unutterably human – I risk
everything, and know my work will come to be seen

as one provisional resolution. Only the stars
are constant. My tears congeal. Ah Constanze
think of my scores as atlases of time, of me as Atlas.

'No money, but a fine gold watch. At the moment ten carolins would have suited me
better than the watch, which including the chains and the mottoes has been valued
at twenty. What one needs on a journey is money; and, let me tell you, I now have
five watches.'

Mozart to his father, Mannheim, 13th November 1777

FLORENCE FOSTER JENKINS

Some people say I cannot sing
but no one can say I didn't sing.

What does it matter why we went?
We *went* didn't we? and packed Carnegie Hall
and were all agog. We'd paid to hear
a vocal oyster, a-flutter,
who brought the brine to our eyes.

And in those moments, so carefully prepared,
no one could deny her
fairy tale role, Queen of the Night –
faltering, maybe, perhaps at fault,
but what a failing, pitched
precipitously between charm
and the unforgivable.

We were enraptured (so was she)
by the whole performance, though I
was never one for flinging tulips
from the gods. But the Gods themselves
gathered when she sang;
you'd see them, enchanted,
bringing a lustre to gilded pilaster
and plaster cherub. Even the caryatids
forgot their light-fittings for a moment
and glimmered, so bewildered were they
by what they heard – a transcendental study.
(Liszt would have demurred.)

What could they, or any of us, do
but smile? – each one of us for an instant
transfigured and enthralled.

Who else went on
against all odds, quailing
and audacious before the applause?
Who else got a poem titled after them,
never mind how flawed?

I

All my unmarried life I did what I was told
more or less
but reluctant virtue is no virtue at all;
now I know
there's no such thing as willing obedience.

II

A woman can love an unlovely creature
and he is breathtaking – more
than ever a washed-out merman could be.
When he crouches over me, reverential,
a supplicant at my breasts, I ache
for him to be brutal: when he's brutal
I crave that woundedness in his eyes,
his eloquent, unspeakable eyes.

III

Every cell is an enigma
of transition, braided
between man and beast –
the helix, the labyrinth.

I long to ravel, or unravel him,
to be loosed, or unloosed by him;
simplified by his slow tongue
which coarsens and smoothes

the salt lick of my skin
till I am flushed;
for his hands to taste
and taste of me.

IV

Shoulders broad as a bullock's
align themselves with pure instinct,
pure intention. His spine, a bison's, ends
between buttocks that have never been clothed.
His belly fur is almond-scented, matted with salt –
passion distilled to a spasm, his libation.

V

No man ever understood how to love me
but he is more than man, and I care more
that I love him than how much I am loved.

VI

I have charms
against bearing his child

    a necklace of sea urchin spines
    a phial of moonlight
    skimmed from Cretan waves
    the lens from a stingray's eye

but my womb makes me clumsy,
incautious with desire.

And he knows: he knows
the potency of his caress
gives pleasure by taking it,
takes pleasure in giving in,
withholding nothing.

VII

I embroidered the bed-curtain myself;
worked till the meadowsweet appeared
carelessly disposed on a field of muslin.
I never was, by temperament, a needlewoman,
but I knew this much: to care for the spaces
in between, and never to stint when filling
a needle with gold or indigo thread.
    Precious little happens by chance.

Now, between us, comes sleep. Oh
how cruelly he sleeps: in an instant
the stars expire, heaven's extinguished
in one long breath, and I am left awake
in a vigil of love, gazing into the drape
of figured gauze, imagining a moondial –
    shadow impatient for effacement, dawn.

Minotaure endormi contemplé par une femme
Picasso, *The Vollard Suite* No. 86

CANARY LANTERNS

In China Town this evening elderly men
are taking their songbirds for a walk;
above the pavements, lacquered cages
swing like tiny misplaced lobster pots.

Air yields to the songbirds' promenade
like mercury – an element dividing instantly
to resume its surface tension – but is changed,
pierced by their substance and their song

just as an ocean is changed by whales.
Bamboo spindles reveal the profile
of an ageing spine, but more than that –
define both emptiness and form.

Later, when men and birds have turned
and returned to their interior lives,
what will remain? Only these lanterns
strung like words on the night

and this impulse to capture or recapture
the moment, to suspend it, here,
low in the sky like a harvest moon
and ask if the canaries' song

or the way we listen is more changed
by the cages we articulate. Silence
. . . silence apprehended now
by being penned in sound.

See how they wince, dazzled
eyes gummy behind Polaroids.
I have my word-bait; they find it
irresistible . . .

They ask for directions, then side-step
the goat's head black with flies
that make an electric sound when disturbed.

I draw maps in the sand;
they are lost already.
In my pockets, desert roses,
marzipan.

They believe words are a currency,
tokens to exchange; that truth
is a solution clear as sugar-syrup.
Whatever their guidebooks say,
they don't admit how little translates.

I know what the men want,
what they do not ask for,
which of them will unsheathe a blade
from a scabbard blistering with jewels
and test it on uncalloused skin.

They will be offered a bowl of milk
warm from the irritable camel,
the camel with inflamed teats,
and they will want to refuse.

They are acquisitive, but to them
bargaining is a tiresome etiquette.

They know nothing of choked taps,
the scorpion's macabre dance,
nights when shooting stars cascade
like grit poured straight in the eye,
mid-day brilliance that splinters
into a delirious mirage. No –

they want fresh limes, bottled water,
dried figs stuffed with fennel seed,
silver, amber, red glass beads,
cardamoms, carpets. Cheap.

I point them on their way
past the pile of lambs' heads
and watch them avert their eyes.

I draw maps in the sand;
they think they understand.
We smile for different reasons.
They are lost already.

THE GRASS BEDS

No aesthetic to speak of,
just a row of rectangles left
to go to seed
in the Sydney Botanical Gardens.

If it weren't for the labels and frames,
would anyone see these spare allotments
laid out like so many minimalist concerns?

Elsewhere, dependable attractions –
the Orchid House, possums playing possum,
the solid geometry brought by Victorians
to municipal sculpture, lawns and water,
Public Conveniences.

But here, overlooked, is an unpicked patchwork
of turf, couch-work pricked out in cotyledons;
a quilt humble enough to suit itself
wherever it might fetch up.

Kentucky Bluegrass, Roman Camomile, Soft Buffalo
Kidney Weed (suitable for Japanese-style landscapes) . . .

Are all these unmade beds part of a plot
to celebrate soft furnishing and negligence?
What could any bedding plant hold up
to compare with the grasses' fecundity,
their indulgence of flesh and subterfuge?

Language needs nothing more than a name
to conjure a mirage, a whole terrain –

Snowgrass, Wintergreen, Feather Spear Grass
Silky Heads, Manila Grass (salt tolerant) . . .

but a pinch of lemon grass will surrender
a scent so acute it's accurate as pain.

If every blade were a tongue underfoot,
imagine the clamorousness –
impressions of claw, skin, sprinkler, blade;
cautionary tales about a frost
that glacéd melon;
and the gossip: one delirious summer
adrift with pollen and moths, brought to an end
by a flock of finches nibbling
till a whole generation was airborne and broadcast.

The smell of hot privet, of mint
brittle with rust. Light harsh as this
is the curse of angels; it irradiates
and rots the mid-day curtains

and blinds. Is it simply a question
of time? No – time feasts and fasts
like a cheetah on the savannah, lazing
at present. Or space, which you exult in

making? Tension surfaces – the *ting*
of metal expanding, the *tic* of rattan;
that slatey taste. Words precipitate,
and the tear duct such a tiny gulch . . .

By now you'll have returned to Bradford
and the Greenwich pips – those tyrants
of accountability, miserly with daylight,
but here I'm sleeping through your days,
swimming through dreams, estranged
in the brilliance of the Southern Cross.

Face to face we're like two clocks
synchronised to the other's heartbeat;
time and again our intricate workings
celebrate coincidence.
                              But we travel –
you among vivid saris; me, parakeets;
and flightpath turbulence, like the pitch
and roll of waves, causes us to drift and yaw,
each inner pendulum, little by little,
describing an ellipse that comes to be
at odds with the celestial procession.

When I return, my hands will swivel
abruptly through the Roman numerals
obedient as a sundial's pinioned shadow;
then we'll agree on a time, will meet
and touch the instantaneous pleasures
aware, meanwhile, of the displaced
days that passed across each face.

Like an image reflected on a globe
of handblown glass, time is constant
only in distorting what we apprehend;
together, our pulses phase intuitively
but the hours we spend apart must wait
for the moment to be counted and recounted.

On Taking a Chinese Ginger Jar Seriously

The other passengers cluttered their laps
with Tupperware, tinfoil, yesterday's colour supplement,
a Thermos flask; I held my arms round a big blue jar,
grasping it as if, let go, it might spin off, intent
on achieving greater density, implosion or collapse,
or falling falling falling like a suicidal star
towards intractable inertia. Some, I saw, exchanged
the odd glance. Did I, perhaps, look a bit deranged –

incubating my ginger jar on in-turned knees?
Who cares? This volume, this feat of spiralled clay
was there to be nurtured, like the very last
egg of an extinct species. Or phoenix. Who's to say
it was worth any less than some old Japanese
vase from Sotheby's? Its glaze outclassed
that cobalt glass-paste Egyptians used for Osiris.
We were inseparable. Travelling was always a crisis.

forecourt flowers and stretch covers
and Dralon scatter cushions with edgings
and soft verges and damp
clothes on hangers in doorways
and putting up with things and people
in booths saying No that's not possible
and hopelessly unsexy women
and men who're hopeless and unsexy
and sodden roses thick with aphids
and the predictable eclipse mid-afternoon
of anything that showed so much as a glimmer
of flair when you woke first thing
and broken paving stones that tilt and spurt
filth over your ankle in June
and mild winters that end in moth
and upholstery patterns on the tube
intended to obscure gobs of gum
and the meanness that lies in wait
at the far end of every packet of mints
and the aesthetic implicated in Cheltenham's
municipal flower beds
and the film that won't wash off perfectly good apples
and the smell of autumnal cabbage fields
and shabby 6 o'clock windowsills
swathed in nylon
with their vases of silk orchids from Bali
and faux Chinese lampshades
and the whole concept of semi-detached
and the slow slow quick quick slow
extinguishing of the spirit
and the insidious self-consciousness that sticks
like a sucker fish to anything with a bit of verve
and the finessing of disparagement
at the expense of (*say* it) love
and the man on the curb polishing his red car
with turtle wax as if it mattered

Up here with binoculars I used to watch
small white packets change hands –
conjurers, palming. Then
they'd piss in coke tins on the footbridge
and cool down cyclists.
But knives . . . that's different.

So I went to the RSPCA, chose a manky scrap,
paws big as lily pads, and fed him up –
tinned soup, bacon rind, leftovers from the fridge.
To start with he'd wolf the lot, then be sick.

I taught him everything. Manners
and that; not to lick his balls
when I brought birds back.
He'd have jumped off the balcony
to retrieve the moon if I'd trained him to.

Only thing he never got the hang of
was the lifts. He liked them Out of Order.
Both of them.
He sussed that one was for the odd floors
(no good to us) but whenever I dived in the other
he'd follow all right.

If I slithered out just as the doors shut
he'd be trapped like a cockroach in a matchbox;
by the time they opened automatically I'd have legged it
halfway up to the 12th floor. He'd chase,
slavering, straight from hell. Drove him mad.

Sometimes I'd press the wrong button,
all innocent, and wait.
Soon as we arrived he knew something was up,
but couldn't tell which way to jump.
I'd make a dash, then halt

and watch him lollop up or down a flight, stop,
wheel round . . .
There were times on the landing
when he'd look me in the eye and growl
before I'd even made a move.

He had other ways of getting me back;
streetwise, he'd pull one leg after the other.

THE UNGUARDED

Two men holding hands in the street, two open secrets,
each nonchalant, knowing they're the self-sufficient object
of the other's love, and this evening entirely content
to make a casual, an almost unthinking entrance
into a night of neon and stars. If they're still subject
to all that's provisional — the circumstantial present

no one can sidestep — their hands are making a present
of it to one another, withholding no secrets,
no pleasures; embodiments of candour. Let's not subject
their mirrored desire to too much scrutiny, let alone object
to the carelessness they exhibit — sufficient to entrance
the eye of a passer-by, the upstaged moon — but be content

to witness it. Simply. Too often the troubled content
of a troubled poem has little to do with the present:
love gets all dressed up and makes a bit of an entrance
only to exit into a garden of verse — unkept roses, and secrets;
or ends up in a reliquary, a desiccated little object.
How many lovers have unwittingly embalmed their subject

in a turn of phrase? If poetry were disposed towards its subject
as we are, to love, would words lie together on the page, content
in their alignments, each noun perfectly suited to its object,
or seeming so? But this embrace of hands is, for the present,
reciprocated: isn't that enough? Only when all our secrets
are known should we ask 'How long can any lover hope to entrance

another?' So many questions. Why cram like this? — the entrance
into the night is free. Pass freely, and let our chosen subject
be one another, the touch of skin on air, and the secrets
all lovers share but believe they alone articulate, content
in this sufficiency; oyster-shell palms, the invaluable present.
When we give of ourselves, no transaction takes place, no object

changes hands, and yet we are enriched. Who could object
to the insouciance of these men hesitating at the entrance
to a nightclub? Their hands, both intimate and public, present
to the street, to the shameless night and to me, a subject
to celebrate. I stand apart: a part of me just as content
as they are – free from the need for passwords, secrets

or the need to tell. How could love discern object from subject?
Here, revealed, is the entrance to an interior where we're content
in the present. Don't ask where. Some things are best kept secrets.

These are the times you know nothing of –
the insistent now, and now, and now . . .
It's not as if I've anything momentous to say
but in not saying it, in leaving it unsaid
there is a small influx of anguish –
the death of something ungiven.

Just now I was watching a silver plane
revert to mercury then recover itself
as it inched across my pre-war windowpane,
and the moment passed, unspoken –
like the plane itself, irretrievable
in a glazed sky, passing into nothing.

And nothing remained, filling with blue
like an eye with tears; only this
impulse – elusive as it is
specific, and the sensation
that quicksilver was escaping me, leaving
an obscure sense of urgency, despair.

JEOPARDY

You know how a famished child,
fierce, defiant, resolute,
will sometimes refuse the breast.

Even now, there are times
when I feel my will must serve
as a skin held taut to screen

identity from the grit that whirls
earthward from each far-flung star;
a membrane that risks

being broached by love,
broached utterly
by reciprocity;

and all that I hold so proud
safeguards these provisional cells,
these granules I know

daren't admit how parched they are.

Commonplace already – chaos
theory; the very idea
that midges can precipitate

monsoon rain in Hyderabad
or glacial retreat.
Clichés always catch up,

blistering with a touch
of literary athlete's foot.
Rotten luck if you're a rose

so blighted by imagery
no one'll risk an allusive whiff.
Except me. Here goes.

This bunch, all hugger-mugger,
is for you; it cost a lot to pick –
a deluge somewhere or other,

drought, or an epic
shift among tectonic plates.
Take it; don't think too much

or theorise. Here's the scent
of albertine spiked with gorse,
and that reckless light in my eyes.

The lyre bird flew in from New Zealand,
scratched around in search of a tree fern
here in Wood Green, and took up residence
for the time being. It sips from the sink,
shits from the sills, and pecks desultorily
at my scrawny autumnal basil. Its tail,
pure Chippendale, snags on the floorboards.

I bought the mynah bird in Venice
from a hairdresser no longer charmed
by its hacking cough and impertinence.
It has a devilish look, a Dervish look,
and a bakelite beak nasturtium yellow.
Picky as hell, it has acquired tastes
and pretensions way above its station.

Both are unearthly mimics. I listen
as I would to an answering machine
unearthed from an Etruscan tomb,
and the sounds that come from their beaks
speak, so to speak, with unimpeachable
veracity. So I hear, reflected back
from the real world, the involuntary

sighs and witterings of living alone,
my tongue's exasperated click, snores,
the asthmatic breath of sex, even the radio's
hiss and crackle between the stations
of the night. And sometimes I overhear
a strange and stuttered song unlike any other
they imitate. I call it a song but it's not, of course.

Strictly vegetarian.
She toys with a rosary,
glistening bladderwrack,
drapes pearls from the lip
of an abalone shell,
indolent, and declines
the soup.

What does she expect?
A side salad –
sea lettuce and hijiki?

Everything here scalds her
palate – pewter, ice blue.
Would she flip
if I asked her out,
asked outright *Do you make do
with lungs instead of a swim bladder?*

Between us, a vase of anemones,
oceans of experience.
Under the table,
my bathysphere.
She stares and stares,
fans out a fin.

Precious little conversation:
decompression chambers
in a nautilus.

KNOW THE FEELING?

Now you're going halfway round the world;
what can I give you
that's light and flatpacks
into an envelope?

Something bitter
sweet; here's the peel
from a navel orange
all in one piece,

the bit that's left behind
when the flesh has gone.
Mercator's projection?
No. One strip

thumb-scooped from pole to pole
and two half globes.
Press its creamy pith
against your belly

navel to navel
skin to skin
and think of me . . .

You're in France for weeks on end.
Every fifth day I unlock your door,
rustle up a little sound among the false
silence, and water your pots of tarragon.
Quite frankly, it's a bore. Dutiful
as an executor, I come here and sip
the thin pleasures of selflessness.

But I am learning how particular
vacancy is, taking one room at a time
by surprise, or rather letting it take me.
I touch almost nothing, but my breath
eddies the scent – warm hemp – of kelims;
only my eyes are intimate with the spines
on patient bookshelves, and scan the space

between things you've handled so often
they've become invisible to you. Now
they're accruing the magnetic presence
peculiar to objects that remain
unmoved, like sculpture in a gallery.
I have almost nothing to do
but find myself lingering . . .

So I'm engraving your window panes:
each time I come I stipple one letter
with an old shirt stud, or inscribe
a word in italics with the tip
of a pair of compasses. Ambitious
with the French doors, a drift
of mid-summer snowflakes and rime

forbids the morning sun its power
to liquefy. What do these slow lines
spell out, cutting across the horizon
or into a view of private foliage,
serifs incised into cirrus cloud
making a fragile permanence from glass
whose virtue is no longer going unseen?

A Hair's Breadth

From this, forensic science could reconstruct
a broken code – you, in part a genetic kit.
Conjuring you entirely, I draw between finger
and thumb your tensile strength, like silk
unwound from a cocoon. Would you believe
the distance a ring will span when thinned
to gold fuse wire? Between us – the breadth
of this blond hair; with it I could tell the phases
of the moon, the tides; could swing a keepsake
above my navel to divine a *yes* or *no* to anything
I desire, or desire to know. What do I want?
No bracelet of bright hair binding flesh to bone.
Less metaphysical than that, and more so, I coil
this hairspring under my most intimate skin.

SHADOWPLAY

These sheets are linen, bric-à-brac
I picked up in Provence; twenty quid
for slubbed flax, warp and weft
meshed like a well-worked narrative –

something to pore over, more supple
for having been sweated into, boiled
in the jam pan, pinced with tongs
and cranked through a mangle.

Come, it's time we embarked:
I have a pouch of provisions,
and this old craft knows all the tides
of sleep; touch and trust a salt-caulked rib.

You want stories? Who could resist?
Let me tell you . . . in Egypt I've seen
embalmers plying their unguents and gauze;
in Java I've watched shadow-puppets

by oil lamp playing out epics on a screen
pinned taut between bamboo poles
staunch as bedposts; have seen the twitch
of projected silhouettes more stark

than any human nakedness,
and have known, for an instant,
that what I saw I was seeing through,
that all I longed for was to prolong

the illusion, to go on being beguiled.
But here on these watermarks,
desiring candour, not enchantment,
we can ask anything of each other:

do we yearn to lose or find ourselves
in the outpourings, the spillages of love?

THE POINT, THE TURNING

Each night you turn away from me to sleep,
as if sleep were some intimacy you felt
more privately than anything you feel for me.

We share the dark, this quilt, occasional dreams,
but on the point of sleeping you turn
modest, it seems, your back towards me

and in that moment leave me feeling
– not solitary, exactly, but . . . unconsoled.
I have my strategies: catch you, once you've fallen,

in an embrace you don't reciprocate, and breathe
your vanilla breath, an essence I now know
as well as this spine which comes between us

embodying what can never be said; self-evident
as a warm fossil embedded in the sheets;
or a history in Braille – syllables of bone

legible only because you trust me enough
to turn your back on me, turning alone
into the unintelligible night.

STAGED WHISPERS

I

SELECTIVE MUTE

Mr Oswald also has second-hand heads and bodies for sale.

Douglas Houlden, *Ventriloquism for Beginners*

I

Putting words in my mouth
with a sleight of tongue

or so it might seem,
at least to start with.

But it isn't always so simple.
I'm not just the mouthpiece

for a sequence of gags, asides
learnt by heart. Or rather, rote.

There are times when his nervous system
melds with mine, and he hears me speak

in a voice that's all my own.
'Ad libbing' he calls it

because there are no words to describe
exactly what is happening

when pulse and impulse synchronise;
when anything he touches or touches on

resonates like a cello —
ebony, bird's-eye maple, spruce

suffused and thrumming as one.
Only I know that later

back in our shabby dressing room
he'll observe his rituals, fidget

with cold cream and cuff links
and shirk the difficult bit —

finding the selflessness
to get his lips around the words

Wouldn't be the same,
couldn't do it without you . . .

too superstitious
to ask himself who

stood in just now
for an indisposed muse.

2

Between intention
and gesture,
that familiar

chasm. Space?
Time? An infinity
of hairs' breadths.

We string together
a rope bridge from shreds
of this and that, lost

threads, and fling it
beyond the lights.
As for suspension

of disbelief:
without the script
he'd never believe

we'd have the nerve
to step into the void;
could pace ourselves

and make it across
forty perilous minutes
to the Interval.

We only get so far
by stringing it out —
pitter patter.

3

Frankly, I never much cared
for my legs. Once, in passing
he let slip I'd had polio as a kid.
Manky appendages; all they do is hang

in there, his crotch, or straddle
barathea – his warm splayed thigh.
Fancy my navy bell-bottoms,
my unsuitable suit? Neither

do I. But who *wouldn't* pull focus,
all dressed up in hand-me-downs?
I camp it up and brazen it out
as if my *raison d'être* were to be

outspoken. Working up our 'rapport'
his fingers sometimes used to stray . . .
I did once suggest a sketch,
something we never developed

in public. Too near the knuckle.
When it's Question Time they call
from the stalls 'What does he think?'
A nod, a wink – kiss and don't tell,

that's what I think. Chutzpah.
But if anyone ever broached
the unthinkable and asked me to strip . . .
Beyond a joke. We know the ropes

and the boundaries of exposure.
Everyone colludes in the artifice;
that's theatre for you. Some things
must go unspoken, others overlooked;

illusion has its own etiquette.
Risky business, defining the limit.
What they want's a bit of cheek.
They love it when I take the piss.

4

Some nights we don't want to go on.
I don't mean on stage – *On.*
A contract's a contract, and we're pros,
but on such a night the chances are
neither of us will exactly transcend

the wooden. We eye each other in the wings –
salvage experts. 'How much longer till
the big break – that penthouse in Las Vegas
with a waterbed?' Don't ask, just get on
with it. Once in Brighton's Theatre Royal

he turned on me mid-sentence, *Chip
on your shoulder? Eh? Go right ahead,
speak your mind, get it off your chest.*
But I could feel his tongue – half numb
and despair spreading, insidious as pain

returning after a dental injection.
Did his comeuppance give me a taste
for *schadenfreude*? No. How could I help
blurting out 'Tonight's the night to recite
some Ovid'? (*What?* But who else was there

to take him in hand, to perform miracles?)
'It's about Daphne. She turned into a tree.
We've been practising on the quiet and
just this once want to be taken seriously.'
They did. And clapped. Thanks to me.

5

Within myself – a density,
a certain consistency. For him
so much depends on openings
in the skin. Senses, like stigmata,
are all to do with puncturing.
So many kinds of restlessness

are trapped in his ribcage,
his pigeon-chested aviary . . .
Who knows him better,
who else presses a stethoscope ear
to his heart and hears the outcry
of crow, cuckoo, mynah bird, toucan

all jostling to be heard,
to establish a pecking order?
Compared with that daylong chorus
my voice sounds synthesised –
no modulation to speak of.
In some ways it's a relief.

When we performed in a museum
of automata, so many children
tried to make friends –
not with him, with me.
Touching. But I was entranced
by a nightingale that twitched

as it sang – wings and tail
three balding jerky little fans.
I'd have spent our whole fee
coin by coin in that slot;
music for eternity – that must be
about as close as the angels get

to God. I asked 'How come
this clockwork bird can sing
so eloquently?' When he replied
I hardly recognised his voice . . .
In solitude, in captivity,
singing pierces paradise.

6

Another resumption of hostilities.
Why should he have the monopoly
on spontaneity? High-handed, isn't it?
After all, we're partners in this.
Most couples learn to give and take
over the years, to trade in animosity.
Counselling? Ha. Out of the question.

Unspeakable. He's the one
who's manipulative. Reciprocity
doesn't get a look in. O'Grady says
Do this and I do. All he ever does
is foul up chances for me to deliver
a little something off the cuff.
Our whole act's just an acting out.

Get him to wing it, or surrender
the thing he holds most dear –
our stock-in-trade antipathy?
He daren't uncouple our routine
from the predictable: it might all end
in tears, with each of us responsive
to the other's nuances and needs.

Every performance is urgent for me;
an audience, live, however small,
and that backstage smell of scorched dust
is enough to bring me out in goose flesh.
But hamstrung like this, what can I do? –
affect a *longueur*, inflect the odd pause,
freeze-frame a moment of stilted hauteur . . .

7

What happened when I suggested
a retreat — a few days' break
in a Trappist Monastery?
The most almighty row.
You're indispensable.
Meaning he's needy.
If you ask me, speech
is overrated. What matters

is hardly ever in the words
but smuggled in between.
Contraband. Timing is all
or nothing; so much depends
on the listening. If only
mouths would defer to ears,
but no, oh no, it's all talk.
I've heard just about enough.

Every Novice Master knows
how little's achieved simply
by renouncing the clamorous
professions of the tongue:
prayers will go on being duff
translations from the original,
or an elaborate double bluff.
In the beginning, not a word;

put me centre stage, alone,
and I'll keep mum indefinitely.
The longer I hold the silence
the more attentive they become.
As for speaking in tongues —
what did it ever signify? Nothing
compared with the discipline,
the charge of a word withheld.

8

And now for a little erudition
from yours truly. Ready? An essay
on Art, Voodoo and Metempsychosis.

(OK OK but hear me out.
Always a trial, forbearance –
indulge me for once.)

I hardly ever get to watch telly
but in last night's documentary
a medicine man from the Caribbean

was sculpting a fetish –
resin, cowries, pods, feathers –
while an American anthropologist

twitted and quizzed
'When will the soul
inhabit your doll, your image?'

As if the soul ever *left*.
As if, at some stage, a touch
of expertise were necessary

to prove some subtle transfusion
between matter and the metaphysical,
or that *something* had been induced;

as if conception were merely
an elaboration of 'concept',
and the soul nothing more

than an afterthought –
a displaced hermit crab
casting about for a vacancy.

It was unutterably vulgar
and I – well, I was speechless
with indignation. This

is the truth of the matter:
matter embodies truth
and truth is the soul,

and I should know –
speaking from experience,
carved from heartwood.

Nerves? Not up for discussion.
There are some loyalties
that shouldn't be put to the test.
What I *will* say is . . .
been there, done with all that. Sure

we came through a dodgy patch –
used to call it 'warming up'
slugging tequila by the coffee mug.
You should've smelt his breath –
haddock royale. Things got so out of hand

I suggested he lighten up – flambé
a belch like a schoolkid's fart
on stage. After that he got a grip.
But I *lived* for the risqué, the kick
of the tightrope, wondering if

we'd overstepped the mark.
Yet. Given the chance I'd knock back
vodka, absinthe, pina coladas,
zhoozh up a couple of Singapore slings,
slosh in the pink, the anglo sturash . . .

To start with it's a private concern –
frozen eyelids, that sourness
pricking his armpits,
nausea by stealth; then

hesitation betrays everything.
Suddenly every gland in his throat
'shrivels as if he'd bitten a mouthful of sloes
and we're left with silence –

the elastic, impenetrable kind
that can transfix a supper party.
We sit very still at the dead centre
of a Yezidi circle, peripheral vision

seared by black zigzags
foreboding another of his migraines;
above his head, a thought-balloon
adrift from a comic, vacant, utterly –

but for the full horror of a vacuum.
I've seen one swell like a watermelon,
a huge translucent cyst. He calls them
memory lapses. That's not the half of it.

He always always gets the squits
after half a dozen oysters –
he just can't resist.

That much I can forgive. But
every so often he plays flamenco
on my jaw . . .

reduced to a pair
of clapped out castanets,
that's when I see red.

Self-appointed Svengali here
calls the tune
and I submit

with a pianola's wronged humility.
Do I draw attention
to this *mésalliance,* do I

ever turn full face and say
'I can see your lips moving'?
I have my dignity. Don't I?

Perhaps because we agree
that precious little's 'good for the soul'

we manage, mostly, to rise above
occasional moments of disaffection.

Having been through so much
we share a faculty – a kind of memory

in reverse, like prescience,
that alerts us to the fault lines

of temperament – obstinacy, despair.
Twins joined at the hip

must learn to preserve
essential privacies; we

blind ourselves selectively
to foibles, selfish strategies.

Our repertoire, our affinity,
exists in oversights, ellipses.

★ ★ ★

II

BETWEEN MASKS

The public must be humbugged a little or it doesn't like it.

Robert Gantony, *Practical Ventriloquism*

I

Believe me, it all started in Naples . . . the smell
of anchovies, focaccia in the ovens,
brine, grappa, sewage.
I was in my element; all around were open throats,
open hearts – the mother tongue's immediacy.

We'd sit on the sea wall where the fishermen
strung up the day's catch of calamari,
and talk all day, all evening, into the night.
No inhibition, and so many kinds of laughter.

My first three-piece suit was a backstreet job, run up
from remnants; coffee stripes in chocolate brown,
fit for a gangster, a cardsharp. Those lapels,
my pride, flapped about like a beached stingray.
Overdressed, we were always too hot, but bonded
by being flushed – young lovers up from Taormina.

Our repartee was fluent as the bloodstream,
and everywhere an audience – responsive
as it was curious – who'd let us practise,
who'd tease, even taunt, without derision.

On nights when the air was palpable –
a broth of tar, hot olive oil, and perfume
after the *passeggiata* – we'd sit on the steps
of Teatro San Carlo and wait
for the stalls to empty, for the rich
to empty their pockets at our feet,
milled silver glinting like sardine gills.

2

A change of heart
A change of hands
A change of name
A change of tongue.

I am what I seem,
I seem what I am –
More than one part,
Less than the whole.

I outlive, I outdie,
Brought to life
By impulsiveness,
Not dexterity.

You want narrative, don't you,
not extrapolation? Enticed
by particulars – brilliant points
in a pointillist tale . . . to know exactly
how one thing leads to another? Well

let me tell you I was reduced to a comic turn.
And cold, despite the velvet everywhere –
smoking jackets steeped in camphor;
enough to make me retch. Even nastier,
the inescapable coterie. Wretched.

I picked up the lingo in no time
but felt . . . not so much estranged
as remote. Manner or mannerism,
my charm was entirely lost
on the audience. Or in translation.

Everything in Naples had depended
on exuberance, on lightness of touch
and generosity; now each turn of phrase
was death by deliberation. Conscientious.
Along came the cheapskate impresario

'Sharpen your act up. Needs more pace'
who only made matters worse.
The English can be such cussed audiences.
Gardeners the lot of them, dab hands
at pricking out self-consciousness.

Nettled, he never could grasp
the distinction between a *bon mot*
and *le mot juste*. So much for finesse.
Sidelong, I'd watch his spittle spurt –
rind between thumbnails pinching the zest.

4

The heart can change
The self-same tongue;
What's done with words
Can be undone.

What you see
Is no longer me;
Whatever I seem,
I have ceased to be.

I act what I am,
I am what I act –
A trompe l'oeil,
A sleight of hand.

Who'd take me seriously enough
to take me to a funeral?
I'm just the chipper chappie,
little more than a figure of speech
even when I'm lost for words.
Provisionally.

But who keeps up appearances,
who keeps on grinning in the face
of supreme ineptitude?
What gets me down
is the *succession*
of hams and fists,

each one believing he alone
can touch up my papier-mâché,
enliven my wire-frame limbs
and with a little stale breath
articulate me. *Animateurs.*
So much hot air. See –

I scarcely even exist
in my next-to-nothings.
But which of us endures
the longer, or the more?
Who sits it all out – a wallflower
at a *danse macabre*?

Forget the last laugh.
What happens after
that spasm, that rattle
in the throat
that isn't laughter?

6

The eye is the master
The hand is the tool
The heart is a child
The tongue is a fool.

The heart, the hand
The tongue, the word
By changing, change
What's seen or heard.

My whole world lies
In the No Man's Land
Between what's implied
And what's inferred.

★ ★ ★

III

OPPOSITE PROMPT

The opponents of miracle, on the other hand, insisted that the body could not itself speak and could only be spoken through, or spoken for.

Steven Connor, *Dumbstruck, a Cultural History of Ventriloquism*

I

Lazarus only did it the once.
A show-stopper. All very well.

But what *really* choked the sceptics
and gave his wife a nasty turn?

Not him swabbing filth from his mouth
with the selvedge of his makeshift shroud –

no. That wasn't enough.
It was when he *spoke*.

Well, I bring off comebacks hand over fist
and sweet-talk the hecklers into applause.

I know exactly what they'll sanction,
when to lay on the gaucherie like an idiot

savant, how much to admit,
how little to forgive, how to impugn

with impunity. Gift of the gab? Listen –
I'm your original talking movie.

Irrepressible, that's me; here today
here tomorrow – cackling, insolent.

Slap me down, I'll rise to the occasion
intuitively, a born-again performer.

Insurrection, resurrection –
much of a muchness. Seen it all.

As for stagecraft . . . leave that to amateurs
preoccupied with talent – that slattern

who'll bed down with complacency.
Watch me – artless, artful, anything

85

but simple. Just you try upstaging me.
I'd con the halo off an apostle, and filch

the readies from a pimp's *cache-pot.*
Irresistible in my own way.

Stand back Lazarus you one night stand.

2

Nights when the balcony
hums like a hive, when rows
of spectacles gleam in the stalls
like honeycells in a comb,

when the workers offer up
the only thing I crave . . .
oh it is intoxicating, sweet
as any alchemist's elixir.

Enthralled by me, they long
for my vitality, my confidence.
Trick of the trade, or the light?
Any old charlatan can make fool's

gold. At best, though, it's a subtle
business; forget the cruder elements,
the retorts — I make my living
by taking their breath away.

3

But suppose I invited you backstage
after the show; suppose you found me
slumped on a 60s leatherette divan

scuffing my lacquered toecaps,
knees buckled as if I'd jumped
from a balcony after snorting coke.

Far harder to put on a show
of insouciance among the clutter
of make-believe and make up,

the soiled cotton buds, pancake
and flecks of sulphurous egg and cress.
Only the mirror, jagged with cards

for a tattoo parlour, Vietnamese
massage, catchpenny B&Bs,
witnesses my post-performance *tristesse* . . .

4

Yes there are times when I despair
behind my chamois leather smile
and arch eyebrows. Once, in Paris,
an accordion being played in the Rue
de Paradis took the wind right out of me:
the reediness, the nasal overtones, the breath
coming and going, so like my own.
In that instant, music spoke
for me. And the accordionist? Blind.
So he never saw my faltering
approximation of a waltz, my limbs
for once euphoric, past caring
how they'd be received; never saw
the crowd transfixed – a static wheel
with everything turning on me
at the hub. For once
my legs were resolute, if fluid
as two jellyfish, and gestures were free –
as I was from contingency. But he knew
attention was being held, and heard
at last the pyramid of coins
chittering into his beret. Oblivious
to the applause, I danced on, improvising
footflight, touchdown, lift-off; even gravity
was fluent, something sensational
while I partnered my shadow,
Petrouchka, my *doppelgänger*,
exultant mid-air. Remembering
the harsh beauty of his musette
and that impulsiveness,
yes I despair.

89

The barefaced artifice. Doesn't it strike you every time –
asides muttered under the breath but projected so the gods
will overhear? Enough to make me hoarse. Stage
whispers. How can I interject, how can I ever subvert
a convention that depends on being overlooked?
Shameless. What if I screamed 'I'm bored. I'm *bored*'?
No no. *Pas devant les enfants.* Of course I know

performers are all executors, but even a dunce of a tenor
will try to drum up a little originality, to characterise.
If I'm ever on TV I'll insist on my own Autocue – a spool
of *déjà vu*, about as impromptu as an answering machine.
I know just how Gabriel felt – the delivery charged
but freighted. Banderoles spelling it out. Like semaphore.

Or think of it this way: a brilliantined anaesthetist
needles your wrist and administers just a little too little.
Conscious but paralysed, you cannot even grit your teeth.
Nightmare scenario? Familiar as hell – my tongue lolling,
mute as the clapper in a rubber bell.

Contracted to appear live, I strategise endlessly,
cooking up spiteful, intricate suicides . . . Interminable.
If only I could write subtitles, or you could lip-read.
Sometimes I'd give anything to give the game away,

ditch the whole show. How can I disengage myself
from these twin constraints – on the one hand, the comic,
on the other, bathos? Cod- or set-piece. I ask you.

Double entendres sap the verve from every word.
See that shifty spectre hovering over there? *L'esprit*

d'escalier. Day in day out I'm beside myself . . .

6

. . . hardly the one to ask
whether life imitates art

or worse, the reverse.

What interests me
is the mimicry.

7

So. Sit yourself down, like Narcissus,

smile till you start to reveal your crowns
and repeat after me *another salacious indiscretion.*

That wasn't so difficult was it?
Now you know certain syllables can be extruded
through a lockjaw grimace that will pass

for a grin from a distance. The ear diverts
the eye, and the mouth betrays the heart;
words, in turn . . . *Sit still. Don't contradict.*
It's not your turn . . . become surreptitious

envoys in a subterfuge that cannot help
but end in duplicity – like all lies of omission.
What do they represent, these sound-tokens
dislocated from sense? Pertinent or impertinent
. . . you and your disingenuousness . . .

they seem so plausible when the irony
and guilelessness are pitched just right.
But if language and sentiment are at odds,
if meaning connives with meanness of spirit,
nothing *nothing* remains to be said
. . . and yet

. . . excuses excuses. How you do go on . . .
it goes on feeling, what? – inhuman, this assumption
of complicity in every shady thing that's done
or left unsaid. Inveigled into a doubtful enterprise
and made, implicitly, to look on or look *farouche.*
Compromise or be compromised – my advice is
take it all, like *baccalà,* with an enormous pinch

That's enough lip from you.
Wash your mouth out with Coaltar.
Salt. Salt's the thing
for rinsing *my* tongue. Like ulcers.
Who's to blame for every scrap
of self-righteousness – his unheroic flaw,
for failures of much more than nerve –
the whole shebang?

Artists, even *artistes,* are exempt
from passing round the petits fours
but he can't kick his bourgeois habits,
scruples warmed over like a TV dinner.
Oh I have my uses – my raucousness
and rudery; anyone in the theatre will tell you
the value of impudence, why Lear
turned to his Fool for consolation,

but has he any idea how much he owes
to me – almost every twinge of passion
and audacity? Not to mention panache.
Given the chance, given *half*
I'd bring the house down. Carry it off.
My CV reads *Can goad, cajole, antagonise . . .*
What does he care, or do, but play
safe, rehearsing dog-eared quips?

I'm his warder, entrusted with overseeing
the daily failures of a human being –
the squandered hope, the indifference,
gradations of dishonesty. All that crap.
What would I give to say 'Listen, just *listen*
to me for once'? Self-centred, he goes on
assessing the crowd's response,
basking in temperate applause while I –

dumbfounded – I who am doomed to see it all
played out before me, must keep *shtumm*;
I who could rewrite the whole scenario
and intercede with a well-timed word
to Ophelia *He's a bad bet, love,* or
Blanche *Try not to taunt the sexy one,*
would consummate love in every brief encounter
if only my mouth weren't gagged with caution. His.

But what's to stop *you* asking for it all –
stars, moon, asteroid shower,
a skein of silver sprinkled across your palm?
Bring down the heavens by longing for more . . .

I O

Impulse, misgiving,
Coherence – all gone,
Like teeth from a mouth,
Like flesh from a bone.

The heart's inconstant,
The spirit defined
By what it relinquishes,
Given time.

Speechless, empty,
Inert but alert;
Nobody's listening –
Was every word

A practised deception
Or true in part
Because I faltered,
Because I erred?

* * *

NOTES

The two lines by Mevlâna Jalâluddin Rumi (1207–1273) were translated by Kabir Helminsky with Lail Fouladvend, and are from *The Rumi Collection* (Shambala Classics, 1998).

JEOPARDY

The Invisible Colourist. The chalumeau is the bass register of the clarinet. The references are to Britten's *Sea Interludes,* and the *Sea Symphony* by Vaughan Williams.

The Unsung Mechanisms. Mozart's letter is in *The Letters of Mozart and His Family*, edited by Emily Anderson (Macmillan, 1997).

Florence Foster Jenkins (1868–1944) was a New York socialite with little vocal talent but enough money and courage to pursue her vision of musical stardom. Every year she gave a private recital at the Ritz-Carlton hotel, for which she made at least three lavish costumes, and in time she acquired something of a cult following. Her final appearance was her Carnegie Hall debut, at the age of 76, which sold out weeks in advance.

    I am grateful to *Eccentrics* by David Weeks and Jamie James (Phoenix Paperbacks, 1996) for these details.

A Lamentable Catalogue Aria was written for Lucy Hare.

Lunch with a Mermaid. A Mermaid by John William Waterhouse overlooks the restaurant tables at the Royal Academy of Art, London. Hijiki (Hizikia fusiformis) is a Japanese seaweed.

Section I, poem 10. The Yezidi are a religious sect found in Kurdistan, Armenia and the Caucasus, whose members believe in a supreme God but also regard the Devil with reverential fear. If a circle is drawn around them, they are unable to break out of it.

Section III, poem 8. Baccalà is dried salted codfish. It is also a pejorative word meaning dummy.

★ ★ ★

The following quotation, about the word 'jeopardy', influenced the way I came to think about *Staged Whispers*, and this book as a whole.

'The tradition of exchanging ballades developed from earlier practices involving the competitive production of *jeux-parties*. In the case of ballade exchanges, two or more poets would create a sequence of ripostes and counter-ripostes, often, though not invariably, by using the same refrain or the same poetic form as that chosen by the poet who originated the exchange.'

Ardis Butterfield, 'French Culture and the Ricardian Court', in *Essays on Ricardian Literature*, edited by A. J. Minnis, Charlotte C. Morse and Thorlac Turville-Petre (Clarendon Press, 1997).